RED-EYED
TREE FROGS

by Golriz Golkar

Cody Koala

An Imprint of Pop!

popbooksonline.com

abdopublishing.com

Published by Pop!, a division of ABDO, PO Box 398166, Minneapolis, Minnesota 55439. Copyright © 2019 by POP, LLC. International copyrights reserved in all countries. No part of this book may be reproduced in any form without written permission from the publisher. Pop!™ is a trademark and logo of POP, LLC.

Printed in the United States of America, North Mankato, Minnesota

042018
092018

♻ THIS BOOK CONTAINS
RECYCLED MATERIALS

Cover Photo: Shutterstock Images
Interior Photos: Shutterstock Images, 1, 5 (top), 5 (bottom right), 9, 11, 12, 19 (bottom right); iStockphoto, 5 (bottom left), 6, 10, 20, 15, 16, 19 (top), 19 (bottom left)

Editor: Meg Gaertner
Series Designer: Laura Mitchell

Library of Congress Control Number: 2017963422
Publisher's Cataloging-in-Publication Data
Names: Golkar, Golriz, author.
Title: Red-eyed tree frogs / by Golriz Golkar.
Description: Minneapolis, Minnesota : Pop!, 2019. | Series: Rain forest animals | Includes online resources and index.
Identifiers: ISBN 9781532160288 (lib.bdg.) | ISBN 9781532161407 (ebook) |
Subjects: LCSH: Red-eyed treefrog--Juvenile literature. | Tree frogs--Juvenile literature. | Rain forest animals--Juvenile literature. | Rain forest animals--Behavior--Juvenile literature.
Classification: DDC 591.738--dc23

Hello! My name is
Cody Koala

Pop open this book and you'll find QR codes like this one, loaded with information, so you can learn even more!

Scan this code* and others like it while you read, or visit the website below to make this book pop.

popbooksonline.com/red-eyed-tree-frogs

*Scanning QR codes requires a web-enabled smart device with a QR code reader app and a camera.

Table of Contents

Chapter 1

Wide-Eyed Frog

Red-eyed tree frogs are bright green. They have blue and yellow-white stripes, orange feet, and big red eyes. They are very small.

Watch a video here!

Sticky pads on their toes make **mucus**. The mucus helps them stick to leaves and branches.

The frogs have a third eyelid that covers their eyes. They can see through it.

Chapter 2

Night Hunter

Red-eyed tree frogs sleep during the day. They hide in trees among the leaves.

Learn more here!

If an animal comes close,

the frog quickly opens its

eyes. The animal becomes

surprised and confused at
the bright red color. The frog
has a little time to escape.

These frogs are **nocturnal** animals. They hunt and climb at night. They eat mostly insects. They grab insects with their long, sticky tongues.

Chapter 3

A Frog's Life

Mother tree frogs lay their eggs on leaves. They choose leaves that hang above ponds. The eggs hatch after six or seven days.

Learn more here!

Little **tadpoles** fall
into the pond below. The
tadpoles swim in the pond
for a month. Then they grow
bigger and become frogs.
Red-eyed tree frogs live
about five years in the wild.

If the eggs feel an animal moving nearby, they hatch early. This lets the tadpoles escape.

Chapter 4

Coming Home

Red-eyed tree frogs live near water in the **rain forests** of southern Mexico, Central America, and South America. They are found in the trees of the rain forests.

Complete an activity here!

Like other rain forest animals, red-eyed tree frogs are losing their homes. Their **habitat** is getting smaller. People can protect them by saving the rain forests.

Making Connections

Text-to-Self

Have you ever seen a frog at a zoo or near your home? What did you think?

Text-to-Text

Have you read about other animals that are nocturnal? What other animals are active at night?

Text-to-World

Have your heard of other animals that are losing their habitats? What can people do to help them?

Glossary

habitat – the place where an animal lives.

mucus – a slimy, sticky material that coats and protects some body parts.

nocturnal – active at night.

rain forest – a warm, thick forest that receives a lot of rain.

tadpoles – young frogs or toads.

Index

Online Resources

popbooksonline.com

Thanks for reading this Cody Koala book!

Scan this code* and others like it in this book, or visit the website below to make this book pop!

popbooksonline.com/red-eyed-tree-frogs

*Scanning QR codes requires a web-enabled smart device with a QR code reader app and a camera.